ADVENTURES OF PICKLE PETE AND FAMILY

BECKA L. JONES

First Edition

ISBN 979-8-9908454-0-4

www.BeckaLJones-Author.com

Story and cover design by Becka L. Jones

DEDICATION

FOR THOSE WHO LOVE PICKLES
THIS BOOK IS FOR YOU!

CONTENTS

ACKNOWLEDGMENTS

THERE ARE A LOT OF US PICKLE LOVERS IN THE WORLD!

ADVENTURES OF PICKLE PETE AND FAMILY

Once upon a time there was a pickle named Pete. He was a wise old guy with a green mustache, black pickled hair, and a laugh that would shake the pickled jar where he lived. The Pickle family lived in the Jones' home in a little town named Alvin, Texas. The pickle family didn't go far from their pickled home, but once in a while the pickle kids would sneak off with their pickle friends without their parents knowing.

Pickle Pete's three children were Pickle Paul, Pickle Peter, and Pickle Patty. They were active in their pickle community. When the humans would leave the house, the kids would sneak out of their jarred-up home, jump into the sunk-in pool, or climb onto a dish and slide into the warm sudsy water. Then the kids would climb up the large sponge leaning against the side and do it all over again. Their parents didn't mind having fun once in a while. But after an outing, they needed to go back home and get pickled, or they would age quickly.

Pickle Pam was Pickle Pete's lovely wife. She ran the household. She had long brown hair and a pretty dark green purse with her at all times. She loved her kids, Pickle Paul, Pickle Pete, and Pickle Patty, the youngest. Pickle Pam always made sure her kids were happy and healthy.

The kids loved their pickled friends in the other pickle jars. Together they would play on the counter or slide down a washcloth to the floor to run and dodge the gigantic toys in their way. The tonka trucks never worked but they would pretend to drive them and imagined the toys flying around the room with them hanging on for dear life.

One day, Pickle Patty looked around the room. She was bored and wanted to venture out. “But Dad, the Joneses left hours ago, and I think the cat went with them. I’m bored and I want to play. That pool looks warm and inviting.”

Pickle Patty’s brothers were playing a board game. Pickle Paul said, “Come play Chutes and Ladders with us. I will let you win.”

Pickle Patty scowled. “I don’t want to play a board game. Let me out!”

Pickle Pete looked at Pickle Pam and he said, “Okay, on one condition.”

“Okay, anything.”

“Make sure you stay near the pool and that cat isn’t roaming around. You have ten minutes before lunchtime. I expect you to be prompt.”

Pickle Patty nodded and smiled as she twirled the lid open. Her brothers asked, “Can we go outside too?”

Pickle Pete said, “Watch your pickle sister and make sure you come back in a few minutes.”

“Okay.” The pickle boys followed their pickled sister out of the jar and hopped onto the counter. They looked around for that orange furry feline, but all was quiet in the house. They ran to the pool and jumped in hooting and hollering.

Pickle Peter climbed up the sponge

ready to jump in again when he looked toward home. His dad's face had a look of horror as he tapped on the glass jar.

Pickle Peter yelled, "We have to go, something's wrong with Pickle Dad! He looks scared."

Pickle Patty and Pickle Paul scrambled out of the pool, and all three of them ran as fast as they could home. They scurried up the side where the lid was half ajar. They jumped in shaking in disbelief.

The Jones family had come home without their knowledge, and they were talking and clanking pans around on the stove. If they had even glanced toward the sink, they would have seen Pickle Paul, Pickle Pete, and Pickle Patty having fun and that would be the end of them.

The pickles froze where they were. Pickle Pete mouthed angrily, "Never again! You will never go outside during the day. The rule is we do it as a family and only after the human family have left or gone to bed."

The pickle kids shivered in their corner of the jar. Pickle Pam hugged her little pickles tightly. "We could have lost you. One of those giants would have seen your green bodies and eaten you all up. That's what they do! They are pickle eaters! I am so relieved my three beautiful pickles are okay!"

Pickle Peter, Pickle Paul, and Pickle Patty were crying as their pickle mother held them. Suddenly, the house moved. "Oh no!" Pickle Peter whispered, "It's our turn to be eaten!" The human lifted up the jar and peered inside at the Pickle family. They tried to keep from shaking in terror.

Pickle Pam said calmly, "Pickle kids, you have to be quiet, and don't move!" They quieted down.

Those big blue eyes peered in with the man's nose squished against the jar.
"I wouldn't lie to you; it seemed like one of those pickles moved!"

The wife laughed, "Don't be silly. Put the jar back on that shelf over there."

The man put the jar on a shelf and walked back to the stove to help prepare food for supper.

The pickle kids whimpered. Pickle Pam let out a breath of relief. “It’s okay. We are all okay. We will not be eaten today.”

They all watched as the Prepper Pepper family was pulled from the shelf and the contents of the jar were dumped out for their meal.

Pickle Patty shoved her face to the glass. “Is that Prepper Pepper?” She looked at her parents horrified. “Are they going to eat the Prepper Pepper family?”

Pickle Peter said, “I’m afraid so, Pickle Patty.”

Pickle Patty burst out crying. “NOOOO!” She wailed. Her screams shook the jar they lived in.

Mr. Jones dumped the peppers into the hot skillet. “Did you hear something?” he asked.

Mrs. Jones laughed. “No. You are hearing things. Keep cooking.”

Pickle Patty was crying loudly. Pickle Pete covered Pickle Patty’s eyes to keep his daughter from the terrible scene. Pickle Patty’s salty tears blended in with the pickle juice.

Pickle Peter thought long and hard about what to do to make sure there was no trace leading the Jones family to their pickle family ever again. Their home had been set in a dark corner. This might work for their benefit for now.

That night after the Jones family went to bed, Pickle Pete carefully unscrewed the top of the jar, and the family hopped out onto the brown shelf. They stood for quite some time trying to figure out how to get down to the countertop. “It’s hard when your home has been moved,” Pickle Pete said. “Now we have new neighbors.” He looked at the nosy neighbors with their pickled bodies and big peering eyes looking through their glass jars. Pickle Pete scanned the area. There was a rope tied around sweet, pickled peppers to keep the lid tightly locked. Pickle Peter pointed. "They must have done something terribly wrong to be locked inside their home." He stared at the sad family of sweet, pickled peppers sitting on the floor with no furniture or décor in their home.

When Pickle Pete looked at another jar, it was full of relish. Pickle Pete pointed to the relish. "Listen up Pickle Paul, if you don't behave from now on, I will turn you into relish." He laughed hysterically.

Pickle Paul gulped and started to shake. Pickle Pam hugged Pickle Paul. "Pickle Pete, leave him alone. Stop picking on my boy!"

Pickle Pete said, "I was just kidding."

Pickle Pam said, "Now do something useful and grab that rope there to pull yourself down to the ground. Then I will throw the kids down for you to catch."

"Are you crazy?" Pickle Pete asked.

"Trust me. We will figure this out."

Pickle Pete slid down the rope in only a few seconds. “That wasn’t too bad.”

The kids jumped and Pickle Pete caught them one at a time as he thought how a football would be caught in mid-air. Then Pickle Pam slid down the rope and the Pickle family stood on the counter looking around. It was dark except for one dim nightlight plugged into the wall on the other side of the dirty dishes and sudsy pool.

Suddenly out of the dark shadows came something tall and sleek. It glided quickly to them.

“AHHHHH!” Pickle Pam screamed. She grabbed for the pickle kids to protect them. They stood behind their pickle mom terrified.

“Sorry, Ma’am. I didn’t mean to scare you.” A pickle man tipped his sombrero as another man walked out of the darkness behind him.

Pickle Pete brightened. “Pickle Pedro!”

“Hey, cous!” Pickle Pete said. He was happy to see his cousin from Mexico. “Where have you been?”

“Well, Hot Tamale and I have been traveling some.”

The other man said, “Yep, yep, yep.”

Pickle Pete said, “Nice to meet you, Hot Tamale.” He shook his hand.

“Yep,” Hot Tamale said.

Suddenly, a large yellow face zoomed in to smell the pickles on the counter.

Pam whispered, “Don’t move! It’s the cat!” The Pickle family was frightened.

Pickle Pedro laughed with ease. “Watch this,” he said as he took a lasso from his belt and whipped it around the cat’s neck. He grabbed his friend Hot Tamale and together they pulled on the rope and quickly climbed on the cat’s back.

That cat was so surprised, it meowed loudly and jumped off the counter bucking like a bull.

Both Hot Tamale and Pickle Pedro hollered and cheered as the cat yowled trying to get the prickly food off of his back.

Pickle Pete and Pickle Pam started laughing hysterically. The pickled kids laughed at the funny antics Pickle Pedro and Hot Tamale were doing. The cat finally bucked the two pickles off his back, and they scurried quickly underneath the stove before the cat could attack them. The feline was so frazzled, he scrambled as quickly as he could to the front door and slipped through a crack to run away from the crazy pickles. Pickle Pedro and Hot Tamale called to the Pickle family who climbed down a dishrag hanging on the wall.

The pickle men tempted the family to venture further than they had ever ventured before. They walked along the wall cautiously watching for any dangers that might be in their way when a little girl peered down at them.

Little Susie waved to her brother. “Jon, come here. Look at these little pickles.”

Jon walked over and kneeling down he looked at the pickles all frozen in fear.

“Eat one!” Susie said.

“NO!!!!” Pickle Paul yelled at the kids.

“Hey,” Jon laughed. “That one talked.”

Susie said, “I dare you to eat it.”

Jon said, “I’m probably dreaming anyway.” He grabbed Pickle Paul and bit into the pickle.

“NOOOO!” Pickle Patty screamed. “Let go of my brother!” She ran over and whacked the boy’s hand as hard as she could. Pickle Paul fell to the ground with a bite mark on his hip.

Pickle Paul stood up and grabbed his side in agony. “Ouch. That really hurts!”

Pickle Pete grabbed his injured son in his arms and the family ran quickly out the front door and never looked back. Pedro and

Hot Tamale followed close behind.

Pedro ran in front of everyone. "Follow me, I know a safe place to stay."

The pickle family followed Pickle Pedro. They didn't have to run far. There was a nearby underground cave where they could attach and grow roots. They could live out their lives as cucumbers without worrying about humans or house cats. The Pickle family stuck their feet into the earth. Ahh, it felt good. Pickle Pam smiled.

Pickle Pete asked his wife. "What are you smiling about?"

"I am thinking back to when the Pickle kids were first born. Remember when the Pickle Stork dropped off our oldest cucumber, Pickle Paul?"

Pickle Pete laughed. "He had the brightest red hair."

Pickle Pam said, "No one in the Pickle family has red hair as far as I know, but as soon as I set eyes on Pickle Paul, he was mine."

"Thank you, Mr. Pickle Stork." Pickle Pete said smiling.

Mr. Jones sat straight up in bed breathing heavily. He wiped his forehead of sweat and looked at his wife, Mrs. Jones.

She sat up and patted Mr. Jones on the back. "What's wrong, Babe?"

"I had the weirdest dream. I dreamt that a pickle family was running all over the countertops and making a fiasco of a time on the floor. Even the cat went missing."

Mrs. Jones patted Mr. Jones' shoulder. "Go back to sleep. It was just a dream."

"I don't think so. All the pickles had names. There was Pickle Pete, and Pickle Pam, and their kids, Pickle Paul, Pickle Peter, and Pickle Patty who was the smallest pickle in the family. It all seemed so real."

Mrs. Jones laughed. "Go back to sleep. It was just a dream."

Mr. Jones said, "There was Pickle Pedro. He was a troublemaker. He liked to antagonize our cat."

Mrs. Jones hugged her husband. "It's just a dream."

Mr. Jones flew the covers off himself. "I am going to the kitchen right now to see if the pickles come alive at night, and where is that cat?"

Mrs. Jones laughed. "The cat is fine. She probably slipped out to the living room for a drink of water. Let's wait to look at the pickles until the morning." She turned to her left side and fell fast asleep.

Mr. Jones stared at the ceiling. Time went too slow. When the sun was coming up, Mr. Jones was still staring at the ceiling. He stood up, stretched, and walked through the living room and looked toward the front door.

The cat was meowing to come in. His fur was all matted and looked as if he slept outside all night. "Scruffy, what are you doing out there?" He let the cat in and Scruffy high-tailed it to the bedroom for safety. The kids were still sleeping, so Mr. Jones went to the kitchen to make his morning coffee. He yawned. He was tired. He looked over at the pickle jars. Everything looked fine until he noticed one jar with the lid partly opened.

"What?" He grabbed the jar and peered inside. It was empty of pickles. Only the pickle juice was in the jar. "Maybe I wasn't dreaming after all."

PICKLE HISTORY

How did pickles come about?

Over four thousand years ago, Mesopotamia was where they soaked cucumbers in acidic brine to preserve pickles. Pickling in the olden days was a way to preserve food for long journeys, by sea, and for long winters. Pickles are also packed full of vitamins and minerals, making them a popular snack especially for pregnancy cravings. Christopher Columbus carried pickles with him on his long voyages and brought them to America where they became an iconic food in the 19th century. Some people back then thought pickles helped keep away scurvy and other illnesses while on their voyages visiting foreign lands.

WHY A PICKLE BOOK?

I was asked to write a pickle book for a pickle fest in south Texas. I wrote this pickle book, and also a children's pickle book with fantastic illustrations created by a local artist, Brandon Munoz.

A MEMOIR
Meant to Be
Becka L. Jones
BECKA L. JONES
WRITER AND AUTHOR
A ROMANCE SERIES
A SUMMER LOVE
DOLPHIN ENCOUNTER
Becka L Jones
EBOOKS:
HAVING COMPASSION
BECKA L. JONES
BECKA L JONES
BEACH HOUSE LOVE
Happy Birthday Surprise!
A Minnesota Tornado
Writer to Writer
BECKA L JONES
The End

ABOUT THE AUTHOR:

Becka L Jones has always been a writer at heart. When she was a child, her dream was to be a published author. In 1990, when Becka was sixteen years old, she had written large folders full of stories and had a write up in the St. Peter Harold newspaper in St. Peter, Minnesota. Becka took creative writing classes and sent poems in to win several contests, and had many poems published in large anthologies back when she was Rebecca Groves.

Becka's first books she wrote were true stories in 2018. "Meant to Be," and "Having Compassion," were her first books. Becka has since written fifty + books on Amazon and her website.

Born in Minnesota, Becka L Jones moved to Hawaii right after high school. She lived there for twenty years. She writes about the many experiences living in Hawaii and the beauty of the islands.

Becka is a Christian writer and writes books in different genres about family, and her many adventures in the Hawaiian Islands. She loves family, her dog, and life in general. Becka is living in Galveston, Texas with her husband and dog as her sidekick while she writes.

MEET THE AUTHOR AT EVENTS

www.BeckaLJones-Author.com

Beach Bella Books by Becka L. Jones

www.BeckalJones-Author.com

Meant to Be (Memoir)

A Summer Love series (Romance series)

Self-Publish your E-book on Amazon for Free in 2024

*Coming soon: Foodie Book in 2025

Made in the USA
Middletown, DE
28 October 2024

62936059R00021